ISBN: Softcover   978-1-7960-5296-1
       Hardcover   978-1-7960-5297-8
       EBook   978-1-7960-5295-4

Title: Lorraine Gibney

Front Cover Photo: Matthew Minucci
Back Cover Photo: Paul Fourianjian

Graphic Designer: Joseph Ferrito

Print information available on the last page.

Rev. date: 08/26/2019

To order additional copies of this book, contact:
Xlibris
1-888-795-4274
www.Xlibris.com
Orders@Xlibris.com

All the best as you enjoy these photos and poems! ~Mark S. ___

Enjoy The Poems and Photos

Paul Farquhar

Liberty & Jeannie, your hearts are full of universal wonders! You are in a photo with beauty & charisma!

Thank you!

1/17/19

Theresa Borrelli --------- Poetry

Photographers:

Justin Jimenez
Toni Lynn Keating
Matthew Minucci
Paul Fourianjian

FOREWORD

Very often, art and poetry are inseparable. The late Lucian Noble Prize-winning poet, Derek Walcott, was not only of dense imagery and poetry, but he was also a prolific painter. And this is because he was a visual thinker, creating worlds in words, as well as worlds in painting. For a writer to be able to create a world is a rare and beautiful thing, and it is even more special if he or she weaves strong visual imagery within the poetry. So, in essence, this is what Theresa Borrelli has done by combining photography with poetry, cementing the connection between words and images, and bringing them to life through carefully chosen colors and backgrounds. It is a special thing to be able to flip the pages of a poetry book and get transported to two worlds, and this is one of the reasons why the reader is in for a great treat with this book, A Gentle Wave of the Quill.

Charu Suri, Journalist

Catching a Glimpse

Opening eyes wide to natural
fluorescent of a blue sky shining
upon my glaring quest, for
inhabitation of that I shall rest my
beak to fill this never ending quench.

Opening eyes wide so to catch a prey,
while longing with time.

Surrounded by much, many obstacles
to occupy Opening eyes wide flying,
sitting, walking….waiting catching a
glimpse all around knowing where,
when and how to earn survival.

Lasting life, never….but enjoying
and reaching as I was left a flee as
a young squanderer. Coming a long
way, I shall stay to the very end
enhanced by what is here for me
today with Opening eyes wide

Matching pillars of skyscrapers
embrace a distance away flowing
water crashing the banks so high
above the historic pointed stones
lie and built for years beyond of a
wonder so peculiar, still enriched to
partake in wondrous times from past
and present, the known future still
becoming.

Reminiscing, portray sparkling
questions to renovate minds so
shallow.

How renowned we speak of forgone
brothers and sisters, follow to
beseech our evermore lasting to
view, and understand as time passes
on. Establishment must be foreseen.
Will these scrapers and tips of
granite so refined change minds in
future comings of what will become?

Justin Jimenez

As the overflow of drops linger on,
a configuration of purified liquid
flows on and on. Listen.... we can
hear, touch and feel these glaciers of
individual circles of water, showering
over in repetitive forms.

Enduring our eyes as those passing
by, also linger and linger.

Matthew Minucci

Seated views left with open distance
goes beyond to be overlooked by
lamp posts, as trees whisper the
wintery air.

Covering over these seated views
of emptiness is the glimpse of sky
blue surroundings altering our
frigid bodies. Let's sit and speak of
unwarranted times and weary minds
around us.

We are but a walking distance to the
next desolate spot where we bestow
adventures, triumphs, and those yet
to come.

Justin Jimenez

Frozen meridians glaze through
open holed clay, clay- like solid rock
where water flows through a stream
during heated times.

On this clay- like solid rock there is a
vision of poked out secretions driven
by time.

The air is brisk a sudden chill arises
from the past generations of all who
have passed. Running rapids up and
down bodies awaiting to view these
cycles flow once more.

Paul Fourianjian

Colors of hardened pieces clashed
together bring views of naked eyes
of beauty, serenity and non-existing
trouble times.

Placed beside on different drafts,
where these hardened pieces are not
quite the same.

Leaning upon another looking as
if coolness adjusts upon to feel
smoothness and a slight breathe
from these hardened pieces tell a
story as to where it all began.

We wonder if it shall ever be
discovered and foretold.

Through These Eyes

Though these eyes as bright as
a moon will glow, are foreseen
clippings of lore and caring towards
me. I will indulge you with my
warmth and satisfied sounds. My
beauty shall embrace you for all the
days to come.

As I lie silently and listen to your
breath, listening, listening for your
call as to touch me and caress my
favorite markings so possessed.
Loyalty is a stamina never to be
forgotten.

Let us sleep and rest 'til sunlight
embarks through these eyes.

Justin Jimenez

Horizons

Horizons far away, separated by
deep blue solid waters.

Trickled over rocks on a pier one
glistens shadows from cold air
dropped upon.

From land, stepping over high
above ground to grasp this horizon
far away.

A deep breath taken allows oxygen to
withdraw, yet satisfy forever beauty
of this horizon far away.

Paul Fourianjian

Spark Tree

Glistening upon this Lone Spark tree
there lies a tale to tell, establishing
morning walks passing through.

Beyond foreseeing that star-like
sparkle and color so fluorescent. Too
bright to stare at the backdrop of this
lone Spark Tree. Formations in the
sky bring wondrous winds of such
creations so natural and intriguing.

This lone Spark Tree shall stand and
grow past time.

Toni Lynn Keating

Where have I floated?
What waters drifted and bounced
against the sheds of my sidebars?

So the story goes like this: docked
here for only a time being until two
Wisemen will climb aboard. We shall
slowly anchor out to waters where
there are many fish, and other beings
living beneath these waters, as will
all these colorful boats next to me
will also travel.
Who will bring back to the deck
the next feeding? Or perhaps I'll
just drift to another side port for
transportation? Yes, I am a transport
also, Be it, my story I leave here.

Paul Fourianjian

Drifts of clouds suddenly bypass a
day away.
Glitter of ambience sway as we say
goodbye to this day but alas, with
tomorrows daybreak.
Soon this bright ball with powerful
enlightenment shall falter
somewhere else so we may learn of
darkness and solitude.

Paul Fourianjian

Calling out with chirps and whistles
lost in the grassy fields.
But why not fly your wings or
perhaps dig beneath to reach soil for
moistened tenderness?
Only your dark eyes know what is
ahead just as you fly away.

Toni Lynn Keating

Drifts of wind blow, to whitening
this covered land, so isolated with
surrounding mounds bountiful
with natures calling of this wintery
frost. Farmland taken away, as the
passing shall prevail these buried
crops and working forces. Viewing
from afar where Warmth ever lasts
chilled bodies.

Waiting....until passing for defrosting
with the sun's ray to continue onto
the next pasture filled once again.

Arise! Arise! To this colorful sky as all embark to reach a point.

Lift! Lift! Drift while steering these rounded waves so high.

Joy! Joy! Pronounced are these unique figures above ground weaving in and out and about within a blue arena. Where shall landing fore-take? Enjoy! Enjoy! All these shaped winded hot air rising above land. Watch as they disappear to a far away distance!

Vision far away of a subtle fireball
slowly disappearing deep beneath
the surface.

Extreme light shiver my eyes
waiting, standing still, of what shall
become, as darkness takes a chance
to devour this fireball.

Toni Lynn Keating

Cool Drips

What becomes of these drips after
drips in deep blue water never
ending time. Capture and enhance
the sounds as we reflect each drop

one by one
or

several by several moment by
moment fountain of all sparkling
onto a pavement as we find coolness
enduring on our skin.

Statue withholding all conditions
forecasted by God's nature. So let's
stare and enjoy this phenomenon
and not just by-pass as we stroll
down city blocks.

Justin Jimenez

How bright this surrounding beauty
withstands all natural being.

Flourishing... only to within away as
time falls...and blossom again and
again.

Shining through all light as budding
grows into luxurious aroma; to
make anyone cherish, not to take for
granted our sight and smells; ever
so powerful, to take away with us
such kindred feelings of warmth so
wholeheartedly desired.

Justin Jimenez

Pieces

Lives we form are diagonal or
horizontal, and are straight formed
assemblies, when sharing circles of a
format, is then spoken well rounded
to see and view a true picture
endured by the words of Athens.

Brightness endows these geometric
figures pronounced, so foreseen,
with gratitude to expand a horizon
never thought about; Only with the
beauty of astonishing prospects. Yet
so close to trigger abundance? Is it
a game of chess, back and forth, or
rather opinions, facts, knowledge?

We are reckless with shadows that
cause us to be untouchable.

Justin Jimenez

Crisp air with natural beauty stands still as a whisper is not heard from distance away.

All quiet in eaters, having a slight rippling affect brings about pondering for lost souls.

We must embrace on each beckoned moment and never foresee what stands ahead; for lives here come and go but we are resilient knowing what adventures, but we must conquer and motivate our inhabited determination in order to grant in ourselves satisfaction to be sure we are content.

Toni Lynn Keating

Enter... with footprints feeling the silk upon our bare feet. Coolness... or perhaps heated soil beneath our toes and heels.

Enter... to the ocean bound forefront where drifts of sand cover each marking. Enter... beseech... perhaps a slight breeze flowing through your hair.

Enter... to freedom and everlasting solitude.

Matthew Minucci

Stone walls lasting yet another
winter storm. What lies within this
once called palace. Through the
structural door we walk into fair
odor and hear echoes of yesteryear.
Standing uplift so abound, with no
other pieces surrounding.

Portrayed by many as just an
abandoned piece of concrete. What
shall become of this little Mansion, is
yet foreseen.

Matthew Minucci

Drippings upon beauty of bloom.
Standing still, with a breeze, lasting
until seasons falter, only to return
and last another time over and
over, not to so welter, standing
curved as this natural piece if art in
nature shall withstand weathering
moments as drippings upon this
beauty in bloom.

Captured through the inner core
where a seed has awakened.

Beauty lies in unique for each
beholder so enriched and chanting
with the touch; but what of a Rose.

Feeling of silk and forever softness.
Sense of smell travels beyond
whatever tribulation has boggled
us down.

Just to touch, smell, brings an
essence to forget all, and embrace
this beauty in time.

Warm breeze sizzling through
quiet rustling of leaves, from trees
standing still. Glimmer with sunset
beseeches a naked eye. Rumbling
through are prey in the night,
waiting to lie rest as darkness is
upon them all.

Toni Lynn Keating

The ruins of Greek times now
desolate, standing high fading little
by little in a span of time.

To only view from afar. High above
these ruins are wondering mishaps
of what was once here. History
foretell stories we can only picture in
our minds and have a cultural view.
We wait, wait, 'til no more!

Paul Fourianjian

With eyes so tender

How wondrous these lights
combined ever so close linger into
one spontaneous staring glare,
glorious to view while shining down
on all these under the spotlight.

Each color compliments a shadow
from beyond a distance.

Let's follow each one which will
mesmerize our minds, and fall into
extreme calmness into our deep
inner senses.

What of...
this elaborate, colorful being God's
giving on this earthly force. Grasping
onto forever life. Seeping to capture,
perhaps rest?

Here upon this branch on a flower to
be bloomed, Ahhh... nature's call of
Spring time air.

What beauty this being enhances
only to watch the next move where
it shall fly and cuddle in another
habitat.

Toni Lynn Keating

Silent Sound

Shifting spirals dangling in a winds
perspective, radiates color of glare
yellow sparks brought on by rays.

Looking through as a tunnel ending
its' cure sounds so delicate and
charming soothing with eyes closed.

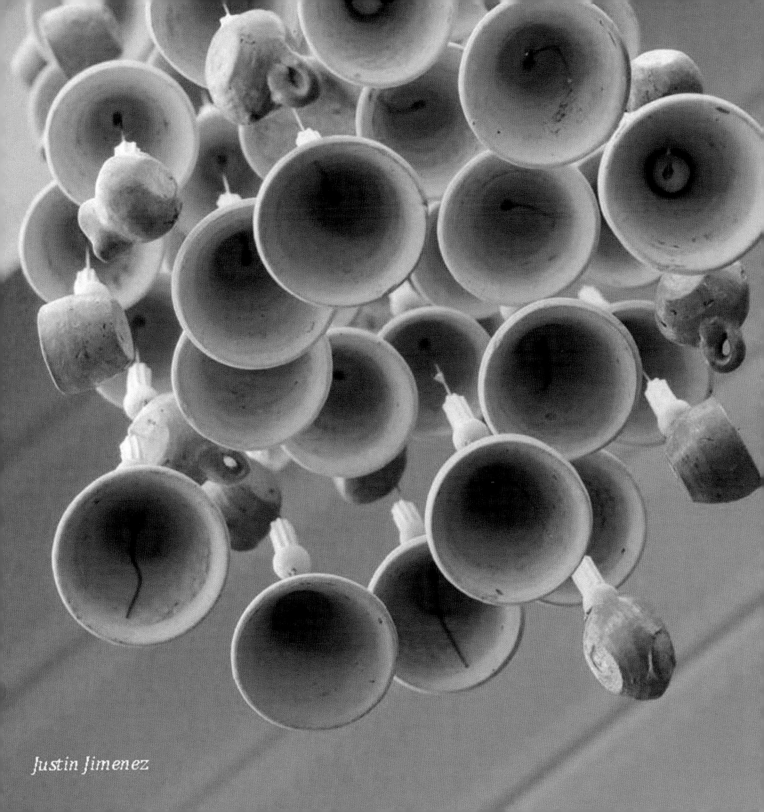

Justin Jimenez

Looking through this forestry with
trails. Viewing wonders that bring
forth beauty to an eye full.

Risking the adventure to lift my body
and climb and climb...

Impossibility prevails, as these were
once drenched markings.

Everlasting majestic color causes
weary tears of joy and bestowment.

Paul Fourjanjian

Look in the shadows of unwarranted
cut pieces. Blended and formed
where only beauty exists, with
wonders, and descriptions of
deletion.

Embarked are the carving by nature,
piece by piece bounces light through
the nights befalling, to be covered in
its' black existence.

Paul Fourianjian

Printed in the United States
By Bookmasters